BEVERLEY MINSTER

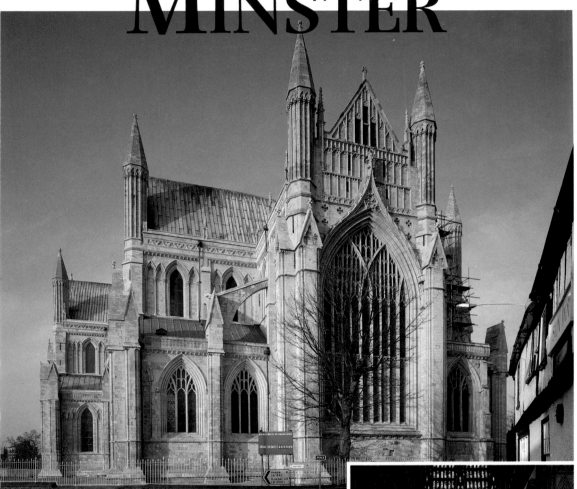

Contents

Above:
The Early English east end of the Minster with 15th-century Perpendicular alterations including the Great East Window and gable.

Right:
The sanctuary and Great East Window.

History Chart

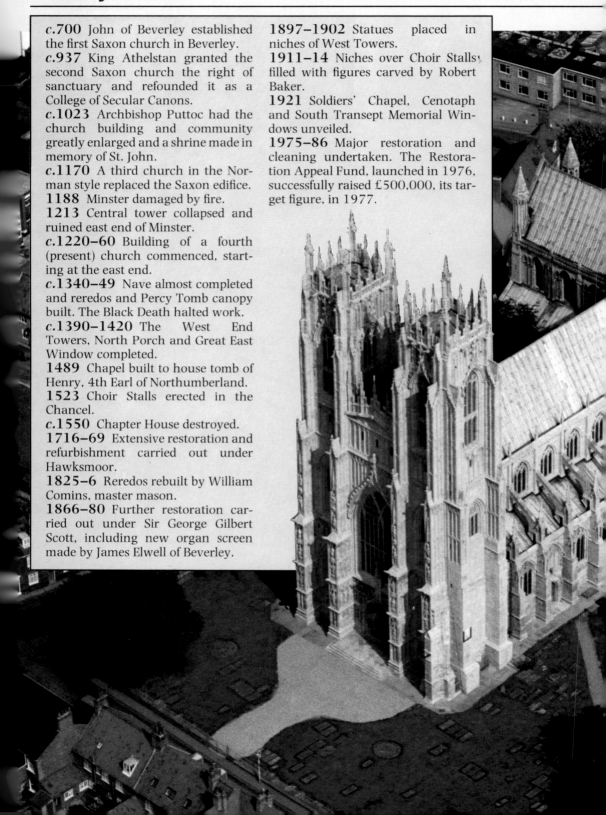

*c.***700** John of Beverley established the first Saxon church in Beverley.

*c.***937** King Athelstan granted the second Saxon church the right of sanctuary and refounded it as a College of Secular Canons.

*c.***1023** Archbishop Puttoc had the church building and community greatly enlarged and a shrine made in memory of St. John.

*c.***1170** A third church in the Norman style replaced the Saxon edifice.

1188 Minster damaged by fire.

1213 Central tower collapsed and ruined east end of Minster.

*c.***1220–60** Building of a fourth (present) church commenced, starting at the east end.

*c.***1340–49** Nave almost completed and reredos and Percy Tomb canopy built. The Black Death halted work.

*c.***1390–1420** The West End Towers, North Porch and Great East Window completed.

1489 Chapel built to house tomb of Henry, 4th Earl of Northumberland.

1523 Choir Stalls erected in the Chancel.

*c.***1550** Chapter House destroyed.

1716–69 Extensive restoration and refurbishment carried out under Hawksmoor.

1825–6 Reredos rebuilt by William Comins, master mason.

1866–80 Further restoration carried out under Sir George Gilbert Scott, including new organ screen made by James Elwell of Beverley.

1897–1902 Statues placed in niches of West Towers.

1911–14 Niches over Choir Stalls filled with figures carved by Robert Baker.

1921 Soldiers' Chapel, Cenotaph and South Transept Memorial Windows unveiled.

1975–86 Major restoration and cleaning undertaken. The Restoration Appeal Fund, launched in 1976, successfully raised £500,000, its target figure, in 1977.

Foreword from the Vicar and Churchwardens

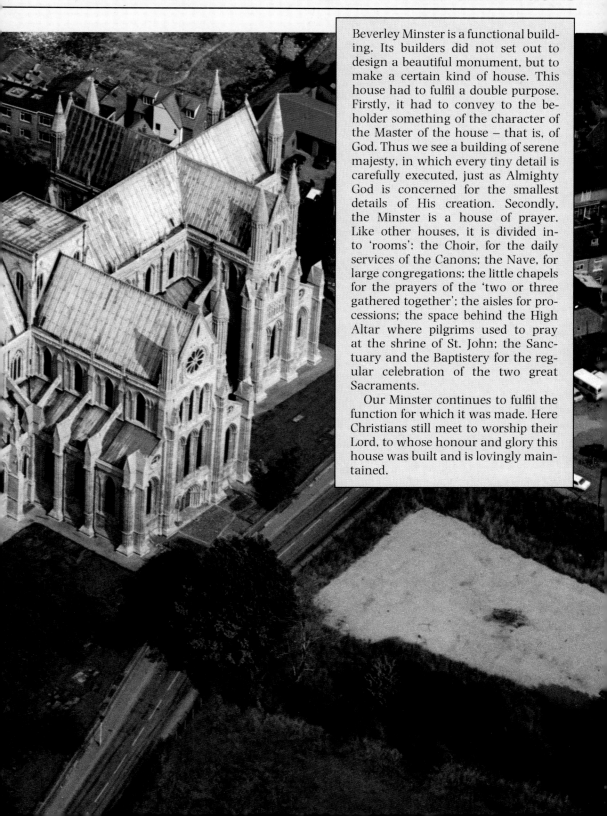

Beverley Minster is a functional building. Its builders did not set out to design a beautiful monument, but to make a certain kind of house. This house had to fulfil a double purpose. Firstly, it had to convey to the beholder something of the character of the Master of the house – that is, of God. Thus we see a building of serene majesty, in which every tiny detail is carefully executed, just as Almighty God is concerned for the smallest details of His creation. Secondly, the Minster is a house of prayer. Like other houses, it is divided into 'rooms': the Choir, for the daily services of the Canons; the Nave, for large congregations; the little chapels for the prayers of the 'two or three gathered together'; the aisles for processions; the space behind the High Altar where pilgrims used to pray at the shrine of St. John; the Sanctuary and the Baptistery for the regular celebration of the two great Sacraments.

Our Minster continues to fulfil the function for which it was made. Here Christians still meet to worship their Lord, to whose honour and glory this house was built and is lovingly maintained.

St. John of Beverley

The remains of John of Beverley lie to the west of the crossing, in the centre of the nave, between the nave choir stalls. The relics were rediscovered in 1664, when a grave was being dug. They were found wrapped in lead and accompanied by a lead plate on which was the inscription: 'In the year from the incarnation of our Lord 1188 this church was burnt in the month of September, the night after the feast of St. Matthew the Apostle; and in the year 1197 there was an inquisition made for the relics of the blessed John in this place, and these bones were found in the east part of his sepulchre, and reposited.'

When the present floor was laid in 1726, a brick relieving arch was built over them. The position is marked with a tablet set into the floor, inscribed thus: 'Here lies the body of Saint John of Beverley; Founder of this Church; Bishop of Hexham, AD 687–705; Bishop of York, 705–718. He was born at Harpham, and died at Beverley, AD 721.'

The story of John of Beverley is recounted by the Venerable Bede, his younger contemporary. Born into a prosperous family near Driffield, East Yorkshire, in 640, he was educated first at Canterbury under Archbishop Theodore of Tarsus, then at St. Hilda's great centre of Christendom at Streonshalh (Whitby). He was made bishop in the early Anglo-Saxon church, first of Hexham, then York. He retired in 718 to his own monastery in the woodlands of south-east Deira, 'having, by his great age, become unable to govern his Bishopric, he retired to the aforesaid monastery of Beverley, and there ended his days in holy conversation'.

John's sanctity was renowned in his day. He effected many miraculous cures, most famous of which was that of a deaf and dumb youth at Hexham, for which he is commemorated to this day, as the Patron Saint of the Deaf and Dumb, and is depicted in that guise in the window over the stairs in the north choir aisle.

His body was buried in the side chapel of his own monastery church, then called St. Peter's, in Beverley. His reputation grew after his death; in the North he was counted next in sanctity to St. Cuthbert. His relics were increasingly venerated until in 1037 he was canonized, as St. John of Beverley.

Early History

Athelstan, King of Wessex, generally accepted as co-founder of the Minster, (the term minster is an anglicization of the Latin *monasterium*, monastery), was persuaded to visit the original church, containing the Saint's relics, in 937 after meeting, so the story goes, a band of pilgrims who told of their wondrous power. Athelstan was on his way to fight the Scots. He took before him into battle a banner from the church and left his dagger on the altar as a pledge that, if victorious, he would return the banner and provide St. John's church with substantial endowments.

Athelstan was victorious against the Scots at Brunanburgh, and as a result became in effect King of England. To honour John of Beverley, he instituted a college of secular canons, in place of the former (Benedictine) monastic foundation, which he endowed with considerable estates. He granted the church the right of sanctuary and a Charter of Freedom.

The Banner of St. John was to lead other victorious armies; it was one of the four banners of the Battle of the Standard. When not in use it was supported by the carved stone bracket on one of the pillars in the South Transept. It is said that when St. John's relics were rediscovered in 1726, with them and their inscribed casket was found a small dagger, much corroded.

Athelstan's royal patronage was certain recognition of the increasing veneration accorded to the saintly John. It established the new minster, and in consequence the town which grew around it, as a place of great ecclesiastical and secular importance. Bishop John was canonized as St. John of Beverley in 1037, just over a century later.

Beverley became one of the principal towns in the kingdom and remained so until the 15th century; the poll-tax returns of 1377 place it eleventh in population size. In 1130 it was granted the rights to a Merchant Guild and Hans House (or Guildhall), only the sixth town to be accorded such privileges.

Minster lands were spared from depradation when William the Conqueror laid waste the Yorkshire Wolds; he removed his camp so as not to disturb 'the peace of St. John', who by now was held in high regard throughout Christendom, in England second only to St. Cuthbert.

Edward I came to Beverley three times. In 1299 he, like Athelstan before him, bore the sacred banner of St. John into battle against the Scots. His son Edward II worshipped in the Minster several times.

Henry IV, too, paid homage to the Saint, confirming the right of sanctuary and the charters of Beverley. Henry V brought his young French queen with him when he came to give thanks for his victory at Agincourt, a battle fought and won on 25th October, the day of the Translation of St. John.

Now or When

6

A tour of Beverley Minster should begin outside. Its sheer size is surprising because, although it is still a parish church, it surpasses many cathedrals in length, breadth and height. The plan form is based on the double cross of Lorraine, the long east-west nave and choir crossed, intersected by two transepts.

Its twin towers dominate the town and surrounding countryside. Together with the west gable front they present an elevation in the Perpendicular style of rare presence and beauty, terminating the west end of the nave with a glorious and soaring finality.

On the north façade, the Perpendicular-style Highgate Porch echoes the intricate grace and delight of the west front. Its height cloaks a private chamber over the entrance door. The niches

Above:
Doorway to the south façade of the greater transept. The round-headed arch here is, like the rest of this magnificent façade, pure Early English.

contain statues of a later, perhaps more sombre, time but the overall effect is pleasingly rich.

The fine gabled north transept is next to attract the eye, a pleasing composition in the Early English style, capped with a little Celtic cross finial to the gable, matching the 'rose' window which, like its southern counterpart, extravagantly illuminates the transept roof-space (what a glorious attic!).

Passing the gable to the lesser transept, in the same style but slighter and simpler, in keeping with its humbler status, we come to the east façade. Essentially Early English in style, this façade, which dominates the south and east entry to the town, is graced with the magnificent Great East Window. In the Perpendicular style, it recapitulates the theme of the West Window.

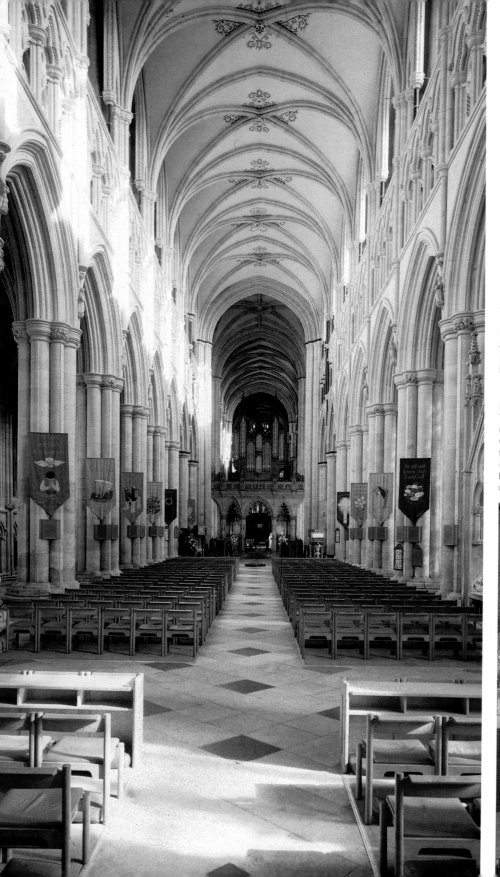

Above: ⑤
A set of four label-stop carvings (*c.*1308) describe bodily ailments; this one depicts stomach-ache.

Left: ①
View of the nave looking east. It shows to fine effect the elegant Decorated nave harmoniously blending into the Early English chancel.

Below: ⑨
The tread-wheel crane, used to operate a winch let down through the (removable) great boss over the principal crossing.

Entering the nave via the Highgate Porch the first impression is one of airiness and lightness emanating from the tall windows in the aisles and the clerestory above the nave. Under the clerestory windows the interposed arcading of the triforium, though later in date, continues the motif of the earlier, eastern end of the church. As usual with this type of church, the east (altar) end is the oldest part (Early English), later work progressing to the west. In the Minster the 13th-century Early English style work extends west to include both transepts, whereupon it is succeeded by work done in the Decorated style, completed in the first half of the 14th century. The transition between the two periods is signalled by the discontinuation of the dark Purbeck marble shafts in the triforium.

The Black Death in 1349 brought work to a halt, most of the nave from the north door westward being completed in the Perpendicular style.

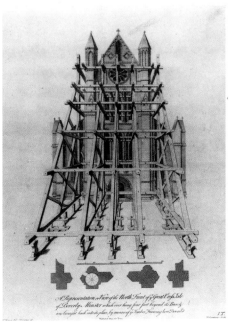

The arcading along the sides of the nave is subtly different in style to the north and south, but, as with the triforium columns and vaulting, the different stages and ages are tactfully and tastefully blended together. Moving along the north aisle towards the chancel (east) end, the label-stop figures carved at the junctions of the arches are particularly noteworthy for their fine carving, historical interest and humour. (The 'label' is a moulding that goes over a doorway – to throw off water – and is 'stopped' by a carving.) The popularity of musicians as subjects for label-stop portrayal in the aisles and nave may have more to do with the establishment of the Guild of Minstrels in Beverley in 1555 than with any artistic criticism, although there is plenty of wry and earthy humour to be observed in the carvings. It is worth remembering that the carvings and stained glass were intended to convey true-life stories (Shakespeare's sermons in stones?) to a predominantly illiterate congregation, and as a happy result portray the actuality of earthly existence in fine conjunction with a structure of enlightened grace.

The great transept exhibits the graceful strength and simplicity of the Early English style of architecture of which the unadorned lancet windows, simple groin vaulting and the use of dog-tooth embellishment are characteristic.

Early in the 18th century extensive remedial work had to be carried out to secure the north gable which was leaning at a precarious angle. This was ingeniously effected by Nicholas Hawksmoor, architect, and William Thornton of York, a joiner and carpenter. Using a massive timber pivoted shoring, the whole north end was gently eased back into place. The last (northernmost) column on the east side leans to this day.

One of Sir Christopher Wren's pupils, Nicholas Hawksmoor, was the architect

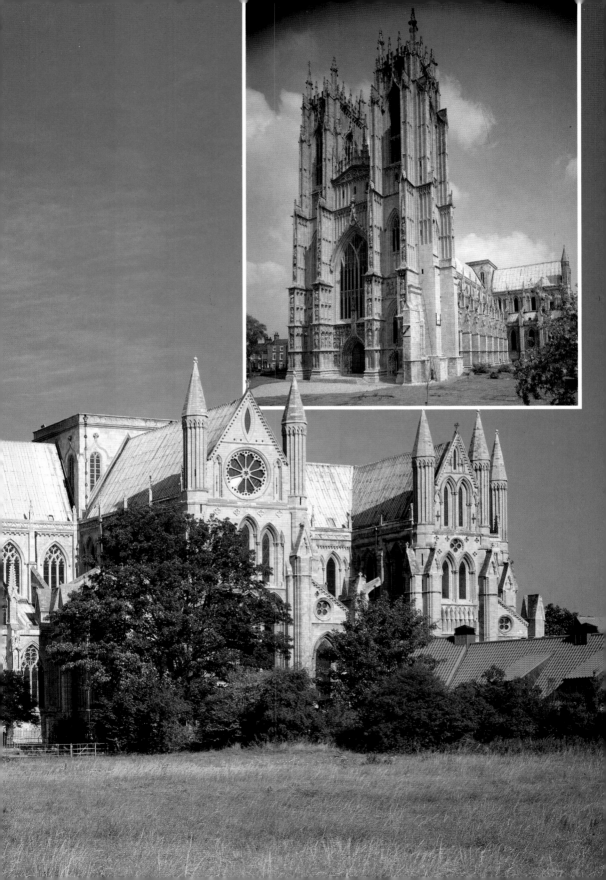

The Choir Stalls

responsible for the early 18th-century restoration of the Minster, of which the floor, doors and font cover remain.

When the nave altar is moved the pattern of the Georgian flooring at the crossing of the transept and nave can be seen to fullest effect. Directly above the circular motif in the floor is a large circular boss in the vaulting which is removable. This is to allow for the use of a winch in the roof-space (which provides an intriguing view of the nave below). The winch is so constructed that it can be operated by one of the few tread-wheels extant in Great Britain.

Behind the nave altar is the choir screen, which provides principal access into the choir. It is late 19th century, designed by Sir George Gilbert Scott, fearless exponent of the then fashionable Gothic revivalist style, and gives a sense of arrival and intimacy in the space beyond.

The elaborate choir stalls date from 1520. They were made by a Ripon family of woodcarvers named Bromflet or Carver. The elaborate canopy has been restored. Of principal interest is the unusually large number (68) of 'misericords', or 'seats of mercy', the largest concentration of them in England. These are ingenious devices in the form of a double seat, in which a higher bracketed support is revealed when the lower seat is upturned. They enabled the clerics to sit down whilst giving the appearance of dutifully erect posture, no doubt a blessed relief in olden days when religious observance was a long-standing affair.

The misericord carvings are of great human and historical interest. They are bursting with social comment and earthy wit. Joy and laughter join stony 'te deums' to echo through time. Lofty columns and arches soar with serenity and grace above, whilst down in the choir stalls, ancient giggles break out behind ponderous posteriors – all to the glory of God, naturally.

All the bustle of medieval life is there depicted: people of all ranks, stations, callings; their costumes and accoutrements, their activities, labours, sports and pastimes; animals abound too, domestic, exotic, mythical. Although scriptural events are popular subjects for miserere carvings, the Minster set can boast but one.

Immediately on the left of the choir screen entrance can be found a misericord on which is a scene depicting a fox preaching to geese – one of the many wryly humorous comments on church life to be found in the Minster. This brings to mind Chaucer's *Canterbury Tales* (1387) reference to the futility of a corrupt pastor and an innocent flock. But in this case the good character of the clergy is not being surreptitiously impugned. The fox in the pulpit is attired in a friar's garb, beside him is a monkey with a goose over its shoulder and behind is another fox making off with a goose. At the time of the carving the townsfolk were being led astray by the

Above:　⑳
The choir looking east, showing the *trompe l'oeil* effect of the Georgian flooring. Beyond is the Perpendicular (*c*.1417) Great East Window.

Left:　⑳
One of Beverley Minster's 68 misericords.

Facing page:　⑩
James Elwell of Beverley made this sumptuous pulpitum to the design of Sir George Gilbert Scott. The parapet niches hold statues of Athelstan, St. Nicholas, St. Mary, St. John the Evangelist, St. Martin and St. John of Beverley.

'dubious' teaching of the town's Dominican friars. This order was noted for its preaching and its Beverley church was poaching the Minster flock. 'You who listen to the friars are like geese listening to a fox, and that will end for you in spiritual and temporal ruin', said the Minster Canons. The foxy friars were seen as unscrupulous predators of gullible townfolk, silly geese that they were. A monkey, customarily symbolic of the Devil, is shown lending a hand.

A stained glass window (now destroyed) in St. Martin's Church, Leicestershire depicted a similar scene as a parody of the appended scripture; *Testis est mihi Deus, quam cupiam vos omnes viceribus meus* (God is my witness, how I desire you in my bowels). A similar representation and inscription is recorded in 1300 as being found in a German Abbey, part of a manuscript of Aesop's Fables.

13

The Percy Tomb

On the north side of the Sanctuary is the Percy Tomb. Superlatives are hardly adequate to describe this exquisite example of 14th-century Decorated Gothic, carved between the years 1340–49, one of the finest achievements of medieval European art.

Traditionally stated to be the tomb of Lady Eleanor, wife of Henry, first Lord Percy of Alnwick, its elegant proportions, graceful outlines, delicate embellishment, rich and intricate detail lend it a splendour and magnificence rarely surpassed.

The pediment is adorned with richly carved crockets terminating in a sumptuously decorated finial. In front of the pediment an unusual bowed 'ogee' arch, also crocketed, supports a bracket upon which is set a representation of God seated in majesty before two angels presenting the shrouded soul of a lady. Flanking this touching scene, two angels holding sacred emblems rest on brackets supported by grotesque figures springing from behind the pediment. The whole canopy is beset with fruit, leaves, angelic figures and symbolic beasts, 'every spandrel contains its figure and the whole is embroidered with a luxuriant vine trail, cusped and finialed with bulbous leaves and serrated fillings'.

The cusps under the great ogee arch surmounting the tomb enclose the figures of knights in armour, bearing shields. The Royal Coat of Arms is carried on the right uppermost shield, and includes the Fleurs de Lys, the Lilies of France, adopted by Edward III in 1337 when he laid claim to the French throne. Beneath is a shield blazoned with the Percy Arms, a lion rampant on a gold field.

The Percy family had strong ties with the Minster, having a castle nearby at Leconfield, two miles north of Beverley. At the eastern end of the north choir aisle they erected (in 1489) a chapel to house the tomb of Henry Percy, Fourth Earl of Northumberland. Commissioned by Henry VII to collect taxes, an unpopular pursuit, especially in the north of England, he was killed in 1489 by an enraged mob at Topcliffe, near Thirsk, and was buried in the Minster.

Left: (15)
This detail on the Percy Tomb shows Christ enthroned receiving the soul of the departed (Lady Eleanor Percy).

Below and below, right: (5)
Two of the four label-stops jointly known as the medical set. These represent Lumbago and Sciatica. (See also pp.8–9.)

Above: ⑮
Percy Tomb detail,
showing angels
bearing a crown (on
the soffit of the canopy
to the east).

Right: ⑮
The Percy Tomb is
traditionally attributed
to Lady Eleanor Fitz-
Allan, wife of Henry de
Percy, the first Lord
Percy of Alnwick.
The ornate freestone
canopy in the
Decorated style is
unsurpassed in quality,
a crowning achieve-
ment of medieval
European art.

Left: ⑯
An intricately carved
boss in the Decorated
style on the underside
of the reredos vaulting
of a Green Man, a
symbol of fertility.

The Frid-Stool

The Minster possesses a helmet reputed to have belonged to the renowned Sir Henry (Harry) Percy, eldest son of the First Earl of Northumberland (1364–1403). As Harry Hotspur, William Shakespeare portrayed him (in *Henry IV, Part I*) as the courageous contemporary of Prince Hal. Shakespeare improved his tale, reducing Harry Hotspur's age by 23 years, so perhaps the helmet story is fanciful too.

The north choir aisle is entered from the nave end through a fine 13th-century doorway flanked by dark Purbeck marble shafts set against 'dog-toothed' stonework.

To the left is a delightful double stair capped with trefoil-headed arcading on slender Purbeck marble shafts. The steps ascended to what was the entrance to the 13th-century octagonal chapter house located between the transepts. This was destroyed in the 16th-century 'dissolution of collegiate establishments'. The lower door led to the undercroft.

Behind the Percy tomb, the pre-Norman Conquest stone seat at the north side of the altar is thought to be the only remnant of the Saxon church founded by St. John in Beverley in 706. It was probably originally positioned in the east part of the apse as John's episcopal (bishop's) seat of office. It is said that there are only two others like it in England, one at Sprotborough Church near Doncaster, the other at Hexham Priory where John was bishop.

The privilege of sanctuary and the appellation 'Frid-Stool' or sanctuary chair was given by King Athelstan c.937 following success in battle for which the Saint's aid had been enlisted, *Frid* or *Frith Stol* being old English for Peace Chair.

The church was empowered to extend the right of sanctuary or refuge to fugitives under the law. Sanctuary extended for a mile in all directions around the Minster. The boundaries were marked with ornate stone crosses, three of which remain on the roads to Willerby, Walkington and Bishop Burton respectively. Like the rings on a target, six successive boundaries were marked, each one closer to the stool itself. Penalties for molesting a fugitive increased toward the centre. The third boundary was at the entrance to the church, the sixth included the High Altar and the sanctuary chair itself.

The fugitive coming 'to the peace and freedom of St. John of Beverley' had to take an oath of obedience to the Archbishop and other ministers of the church, to be of good behaviour, to give details of his misdemeanours, and a fee. This entitled him to board, lodging and protection for thirty days and nights, as well as the good offices of the canons in reconciliation with his pursuers. If such attempts failed he was given safe escort out of the locality. This process could be repeated, but the third request required lifelong service to the church.

Detailed records were kept; the register for the years 1478–1539 survives to show that 469 self-confessed criminals sought sanctuary during those years. Privileges were greatly reduced at the Reformation, and ended at Beverley (and with certain exceptions were generally abolished) in 1540.

Left: (17)
The Frid-Stool. This stone seat near the altar was endowed with the right of sanctuary by King Athelstan c.937 (*Frid Stol* is Old English for Peace Chair). It is possibly the only remains of the Saxon Church founded by Saint John of Beverley in 706 and was probably his episcopal seat.

Above:
An early 19th-century drawing of a sanctuary cross.

Right: (14)
In the foreground are the 18th-century gates formerly at the entrance to the choir. The fine Early English double stair on the right originally gave access via a double door to a raised 13th-century octagonal Chapter House (demolished 1550). The door under the landing led to the sacristy.

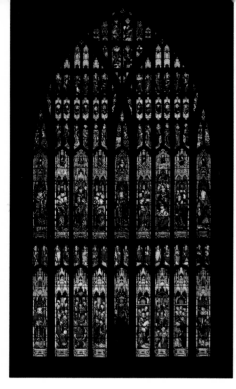

The Great West Door was executed in its present form under the direction of Nicholas Hawksmoor as part of his restoration of the Minster in the early years of the 18th century, and was restored by Sir George Gilbert Scott around 1865 (when, incidentally, bullets were found embedded in the doors, a legacy of Civil War skirmishes).

The figures on the doors are of the four evangelist saints over the four living creatures seen by St. John before the throne of God. An angel is to be seen under St. Matthew, a lion below St. Mark, an ox beneath St. Luke and an eagle below St. John. The Georgian carving suggests earlier continental influence.

Next to the south door is the Norman font. The exuberant ornament of the font cover (dating from 1721) clearly associates it with the contemporary west doors. The font beneath is much older, a fine example of late Norman carving, c.1170. The ponderous mass of Frosterley marble is relieved by an elegant arcading motif inscribed round the bowl, a stem of clustered shafts and clawed feet, the whole being suitably raised on a stepped podium. The font is a legacy of

the original Norman church which in turn succeeded the Saxon one. Surprisingly little survives from the Norman period, the only other remains being some Norman stonework which can be found in the south aisle wall further east and in the arcading in the roof above the south aisle.

Nearby, on each side of the south door, are two cast-lead figures. They came originally from either side of the 18th-century choir screen and represent the founders of the Minster, St. John of Beverley and King Athelstan.

Situated between two pillars in the south aisle of the nave is a 14th-century canopied tomb. The 'Two Sisters' tomb is reputed to be the burial place of two spinster sisters who donated land to the town. Its simple elegance makes a pleasing foil to the richness of the Percy Tomb in the north choir aisle.

The three bays of the eastern aisle of the southern arm of the Great Transept are kept as memorial chapels. The 'Henin Cross' displayed in the first bay was erected by the soldiers themselves in

Above: ①
The carved oak figures on the Great West Door represent the four evangelists Matthew, Mark, Luke and John (from right to left) with their symbols beneath. The cherub heads between represent the four seasons.

Above, left: ①
The Great West Window is Perpendicular in style, like the Great East Window. The Victorian stained glass portraying scenes of the early history of Christianity in Northumbria was installed by public subscription (1859–1861).

Above:
he Norman font
.1170, has an
laborately carved
8th-century cover.
he cast-lead figures
f St. John of Beverley
nd King Athelstan
an be seen on the
ight.

1917 at Henin Hill, near Arras, in memory of their fallen comrades, after they had broken through the Hindenburg Line at that place.

A Cenotaph in the central bay, modelled on the tomb of King Edward the Confessor in Westminster Abbey, commemorates the officers and men of the East Yorkshire Regiment who died in the First World War.

The retrochoir at the eastern extremity of the Minster is notable for the fine Perpendicular East Window containing fragments of medieval glass with 19th-century additions. The side walls have central Early English lancet windows with blank arches on each side. The back of the reredos or altar screen facing the Great East Window consists of three arches on clustered shafts with elaborate 14th-century flamboyant tracery and exquisitely carved canopies. The bosses of the vaulting are adorned with undercut leaf and animal motifs.